Snacks & Appetizers

Salads & Sides

Soups & Main Dishes

Snacks & Appetizers

SPICED · HOLIDAY · PECANS

SUGAR

Cayenne Pepper

Nutmeg

4

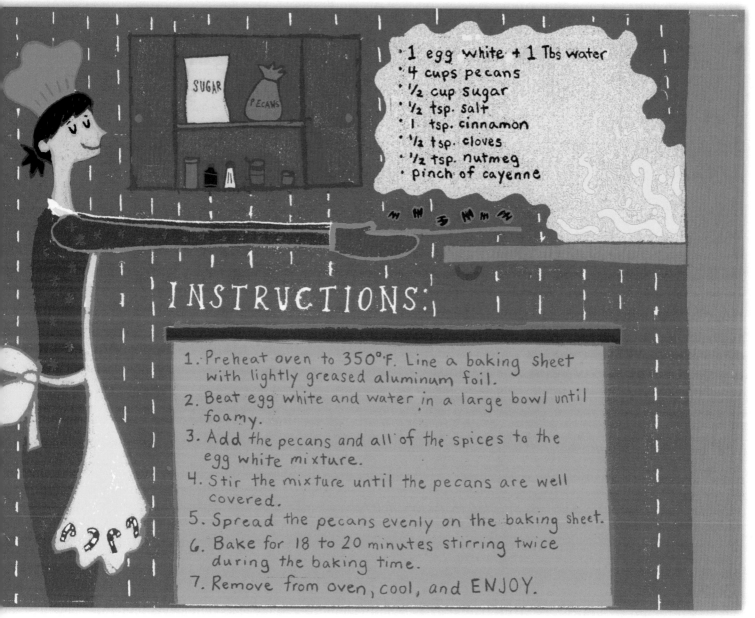

- 1 egg white + 1 Tbs water
- 4 cups pecans
- ½ cup sugar
- ½ tsp. salt
- 1 tsp. cinnamon
- ½ tsp. cloves
- ½ tsp. nutmeg
- pinch of cayenne

INSTRUCTIONS:

1. Preheat oven to 350°F. Line a baking sheet with lightly greased aluminum foil.
2. Beat egg white and water in a large bowl until foamy.
3. Add the pecans and all of the spices to the egg white mixture.
4. Stir the mixture until the pecans are well covered.
5. Spread the pecans evenly on the baking sheet.
6. Bake for 18 to 20 minutes stirring twice during the baking time.
7. Remove from oven, cool, and ENJOY.

Spiced Holiday Pecans by Kathleen Marcotte from Chicago, IL (kathleenmarcotte.com)

1/2 Cup
Kalamata
Olives
diced.

2 Tbsp. Basil
finely chopped

2/3 cup
sundried tomatos
chopped

2 Tbsp.
Parsley
finely
chopped

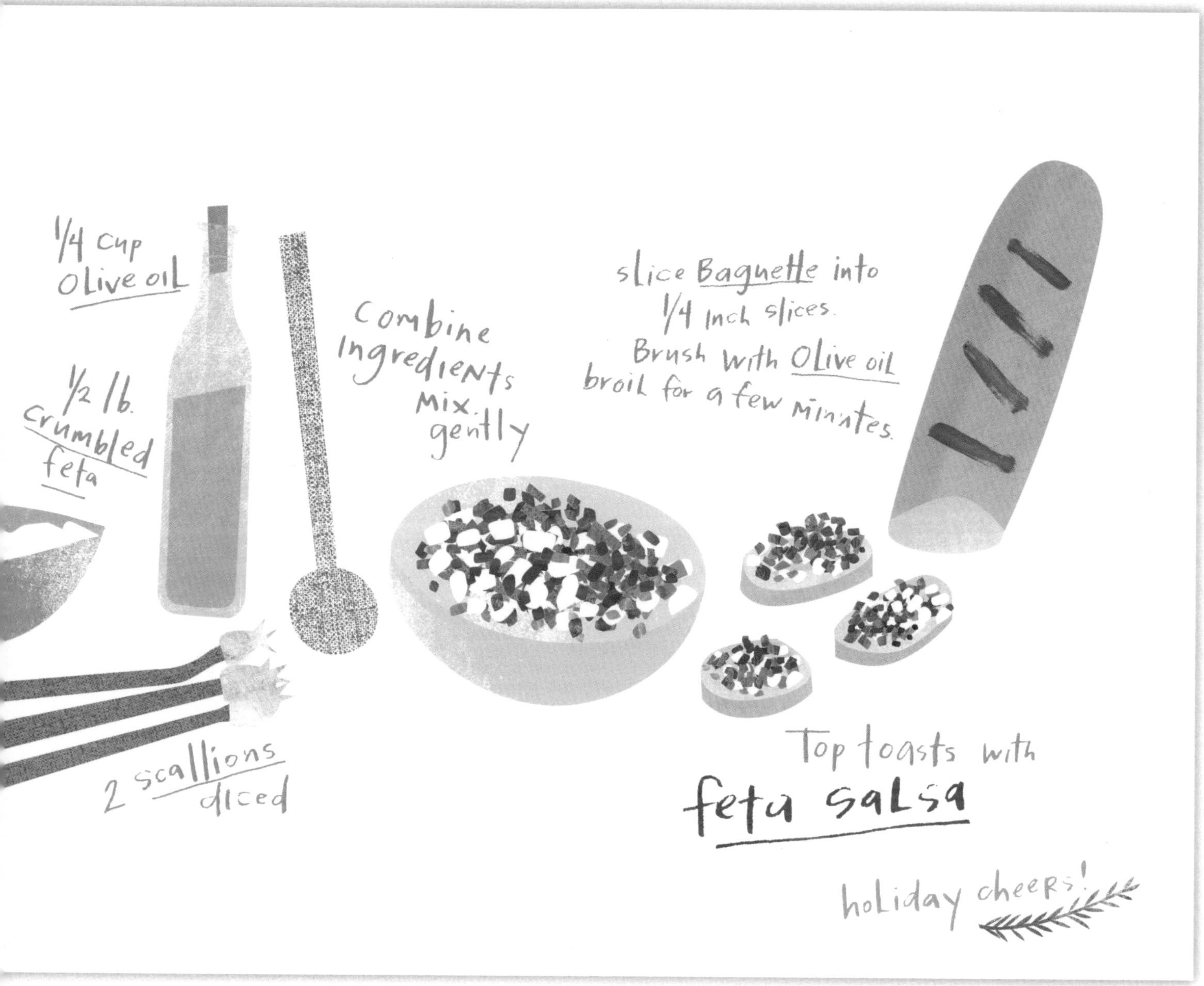

1/4 cup Olive oil
1/2 lb. crumbled feta
2 scallions diced
Combine Ingredients Mix. gently
slice Baguette into 1/4 inch slices.
Brush with Olive oil
broil for a few minutes.
Top toasts with
feta salsa
holiday cheers!

Feta Salsa by Heidi Schweigert from Minneapolis, MN (heidischweigert.com)

Red and Green Snacks

oh so delicious and healthy too! ♥

cherry
tomatoes

basil
leaves
drizzle with
vinagerette

broccoli
dipped in
low-fat
dressing

Red and Green Snacks by Sharon Mann from Las Vegas, NV (sharonmanndesigns.com)

I like my almonds like I like my friends- sweet AND spicy.

SPICED ALMONDS

That's nuts!

5 cups of whole almonds
1/2 c. sugar
3 tsp. sea salt
2 tsp. cayenne pepper

2 tbsp. honey
2 tsp. vegetable oil
2 tbsp. water

Preheat oven to 350 degrees. Spread almonds out on a cookie sheet or two and roast for 10 minutes.

In a large bowl combine sugar, salt and cayenne.

In a large skillet, cook honey, oil and water over medium heat. Add almonds, toss to coat.

Drain and transfer almonds to sugar mix. Toss to coat.

Spread almonds onto wax paper and let cool. Can be stored for up to 2 weeks in airtight container.

I feel pretty, oh so pretty...

ALMONDS ARE MAGIC!
✓ Good for your brain
✓ Regulates cholesterol
✓ Good for your heart
✓ Improves complexion
✓ Regulates blood pressure
✓ Prevents colon cancer
✓ Protection from diabetes
✓ Beneficial for baby
✓ Helps weight loss
✓ Prevents constipation
✓ Boosts energy

TO·YOU!
LOVE·ME!

HAPPY HOLiDAYS

wrap in fancy bag and ribbon and give to all your nutty friends.

Spiced Almonds by Lisa Graves from Medway, MA (lisagravesdesign.blogspot.com)

Green

White

PUFF PASTRY

SESAME

1 SHEET

Cut the puff pastry with Christmas biscuit cutters. Brush all pastry shapes with milk and then add sesame on the top. Bake on parchment paper.

A PLATE WITH A BIT OF MILK

BISCUIT CUTTERS

2/3 CUP OIL

4 OZ. ARUGULA

Put arugula and half oil into food processor bowl and mix slowly for few minutes. Add the remaining oil, salt, parmesan cheese and pine nuts. Continue to mix until you have a homogeneous mixture

SALT

2 PINCHES

PINE NUTS

1/2 CUP

2/3 CUP GRATED

PARMESAN CHEESE

& Red

SOME CHERRY TOMATOES CUT IN TWO

SLICED MOZZARELLA CHEESE

When the pastry shapes are cold, cover with a teaspoon of arugula pesto. Add a mozzarella cheese slice and then half cherry tomato. Enjoy your appetizer!

Green White & Red by Silvia Sponza from Milan, Italy (be.net/silviasponza)   13

1. Cut off the top and the bottom.

2. Lay flat.

3. Make four cuts around the outside.

4. Make four diamond-shaped cuts in the middle.

5. Criss-cross cuts in the center.

Radish

6. Soak in ice water until the petals open.

Roses

the *Posh*

zucchini

tart

Crust

- 1 cup flour
- 1/2 cup wholemeal flour
- 1/2 cup butter
- 1 Egg yolk
- 1 Tsp. salt
- Ice water
  (helps dough hold together)

Knead dough and roll it up.
Place onto a pie plate.
Chill it in fridge.

Sauté

1 medium sized onion
1 medium sized red pepper ⎫ well
2 to 3 garlic cloves ⎬ chopped

Slice and add

3 to 4 zucchinis. Salt
Toss all the veggies together
but dont overcook.
Let it cool and stir in an egg.
*Optional: some creamy cheese
or 1/2 cup cream.*

Spice it up!

Add
Fresh ginger. Freshly ground pepper
Freshly grated parmeggian cheese.
Fill in the <u>uncooked</u> pie crust and arrange
sliced fresh mushrooms on top.
Sprinkle some more parmeggian cheese.

Cook !

**Oven 370 ° F
Around 40 min.**

The Posh (Zucchini) Tart by Nathalie Beauvois from Solymar, Uruguay (nathaliebeauvois.weebly.com)   17

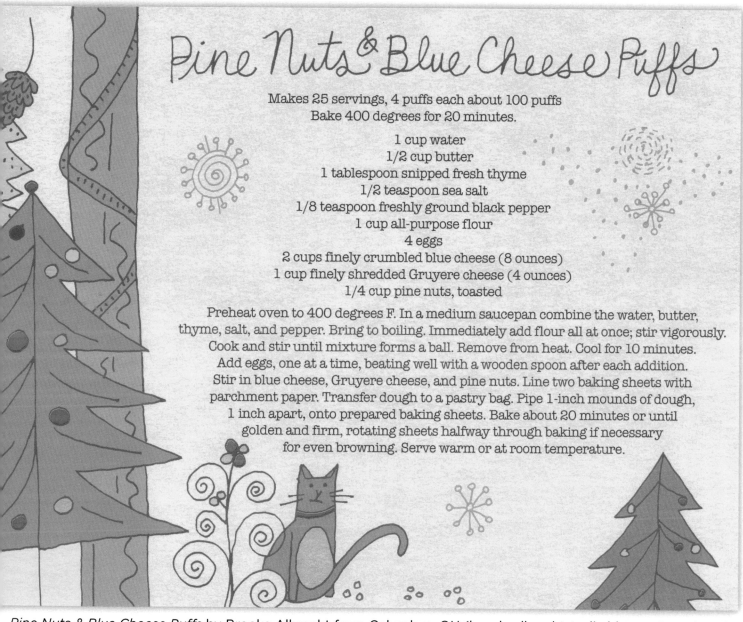

Pine Nuts & Blue Cheese Puffs

Makes 25 servings, 4 puffs each about 100 puffs
Bake 400 degrees for 20 minutes.

1 cup water
1/2 cup butter
1 tablespoon snipped fresh thyme
1/2 teaspoon sea salt
1/8 teaspoon freshly ground black pepper
1 cup all-purpose flour
4 eggs
2 cups finely crumbled blue cheese (8 ounces)
1 cup finely shredded Gruyere cheese (4 ounces)
1/4 cup pine nuts, toasted

Preheat oven to 400 degrees F. In a medium saucepan combine the water, butter, thyme, salt, and pepper. Bring to boiling. Immediately add flour all at once; stir vigorously. Cook and stir until mixture forms a ball. Remove from heat. Cool for 10 minutes. Add eggs, one at a time, beating well with a wooden spoon after each addition. Stir in blue cheese, Gruyere cheese, and pine nuts. Line two baking sheets with parchment paper. Transfer dough to a pastry bag. Pipe 1-inch mounds of dough, 1 inch apart, onto prepared baking sheets. Bake about 20 minutes or until golden and firm, rotating sheets halfway through baking if necessary for even browning. Serve warm or at room temperature.

Pine Nuts & Blue Cheese Puffs by Brooke Albrecht from Columbus, OH (brookealbrechtstudio.blogspot.com)

Salads & Sides

combine fruit

Jeweled
Fruit Salad

one
sectioned
blood orange

one
sliced
pear

toss with dressing

seeds of one pomegranate

two sliced mangos

half cup julienned jicama

equal parts lime & honey juice

two-sectioned tangerines

ground red pepper and sea salt

six sliced kumquats

Jeweled Fruit Salad by Jessica Flannery from Boston, MA (jflannerydesign.com)   23

Miss Phyllis "Success" Cranberry Mold

Fancy Dishes

Silver Service

Vintage Cake Stand

Silverware

After years of Refinement

Combine · Boil (15 min).

Dice, Peel 1 Fuji Apple

12 oz fresh Cranberries &

Pour into Mold.

Cool to Firm.

3/4 c. Water

1 c. Sugar

More Fancy Dishes

Wrinkle-free

beautiful hair

THIS SALAD IS FULL OF VITAMIN
C AND OTHER ANTI-OXIDANTS
TO KEEP YOUR SKIN CLEAR
& YOUR COLLAGEN STRONG!

2 TBSP EXTRA-VIRGIN OLIVE OIL
1 TBSP BALSAMIC VINEGAR
1 TSP SEA SALT
FRESHLY GROUND WHITE PEPPER
1½ LBS ZUCCHINI-PEELED &
   SLICED LENGTHWISE 1/8 INCH THICK
1 LB ASPARAGUS TRIMMED
¼ CUP FRESHLY CHOPPED PARSLEY
¼ CUP FRESHLY CHOPPED BASIL
4 OZ GOAT CHEESE OR FETA
      CHEESE-CRUMBLED
ZEST & JUICE OF 1 LEMON

PREHEAT GRILL-PAN ON STOVE
ONE TO TWO MINUTES. COMBINE
OIL, VINEGAR, SEA SALT & PEPPER
IN BOWL. GRILL VEGETABLES IN
PREHEATED PAN FOR A FEW MINUTES
ON EACH SIDE UNTIL SLIGHTLY
BROWN. TRANSFER VEGETABLES
TO A SERVING DISH. SPRINKLE
WITH PARSLEY, BASIL, GOAT'S
CHEESE OR FETA CHEESE, LEMON ZEST
& JUICE. TASTE AND ADJUST SEASONINGS
IF NECESSARY BEFORE SERVING.
   SERVES FOUR TO SIX

AnTi-Aging Salad
with Zucchini & ASparagus

Santa's Anti-Aging Salad by Jean Cameron from Amsterdam, The Netherlands (jeanc.nl)

PINK SALAD

1 BEETROOT (PRE-COOKED)

1 TABLESPOON OF GREEK YOGURT OR QUARK

A SQUEEZE OF LEMON JUICE

SALT

PEPPER

1 TEASPOON OF MAYO

A FEW LEAVES OF MINT CHOPPED

A HANDFUL OF ROASTED SESAME SEEDS

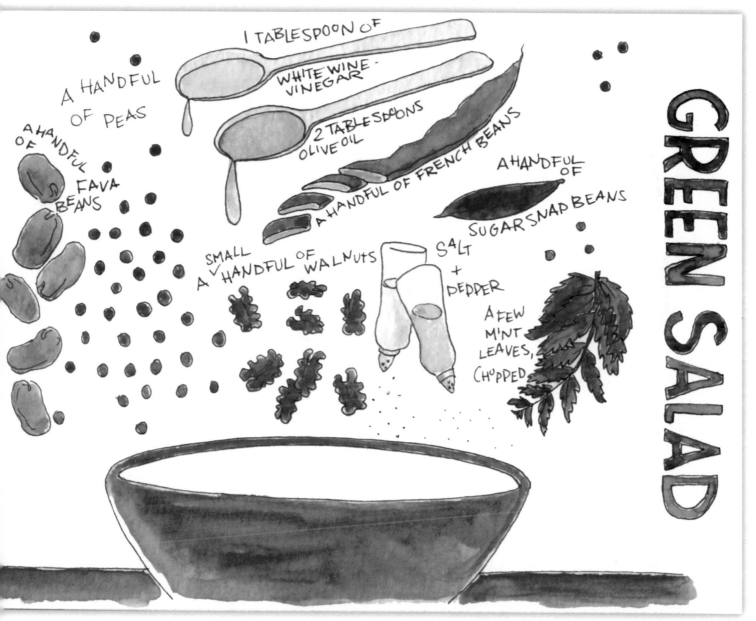

GREEN SALAD

A HANDFUL OF PEAS

1 TABLESPOON OF WHITE WINE VINEGAR

A HANDFUL OF FAVA BEANS

2 TABLESPOONS OLIVE OIL

A HANDFUL OF FRENCH BEANS

A HANDFUL OF SUGAR SNAP BEANS

A SMALL HANDFUL OF WALNUTS

SALT + PEPPER

A FEW MINT LEAVES, CHOPPED

Pomegranate Pear Máche Walnut Salad by Salli Swindell from Hudson, OH (studiosss.tumblr.com)

MASHED POTATO MOUNTAIN

Ingredients

5 lbs Russet/Yukon potatoes, peeled
2 sticks salted butter, softened
8 oz cream cheese, softened
1/4 cup heavy cream (or more)
1 ts each salt & pepper, to taste

Easy Steps

1. Peel and cut potatoes in golf ball sized pieces.
2. Boil them for around 30 minutes, until a fork easily pokes into them.
3. Drain in a colander, then place them back into the dry pot.
4. Put the pot on the stove and mash the potatoes while on low heat.
5. Add 1 1/2 stick of butter, all the cream cheese and the cream.
6. Mash it all up, then mix in the salt and pepper.
7. Transfer to a baking dish, top with a several slabs of butter.
8. When you're ready to serve, bake at 350° til it's all warmed up again.

Chop cabbage and apples and boil them together.

raisins

1 red cabbage

garlic

2 russet apple

Strain and
toss in olive oil
with garlic
and
raisins

ChristmasRed Cabbage

Christmas Red Cabbage by Mayte Sánchez Sempere from Madrid, Spain (maytesanchez.blogspot.com)

ROASTED VEGETABLES

1

2 CUT THE VEGETABLES

OLIVE OIL

OIL THE BAKING TRAY

THIN SLICES

3

SPRINKLE WITH SALT AND PLACE
A FEW SPRIGS OF ROSEMARY ON TOP

AND PLACE THEM ON THE
TRAY CUT-SIDE DOWN

YAM

WASH VEGETABLES

PUMPKIN

POTATO

DON'T PEEL IT

GARLIC

BAKE IT
40 MINUTES

AT 375° F

CARROT

ENJOY!

IT'S A GREAT SIDE DISH FOR MEAT, FISH, OR AS A VEGETARIAN
ENTREE WITH SALAD AND A FRESH YOGURT SAUCE.

Roasted Vegetables by Miro Poferl from Munich, Germany (heymiro.de) 37

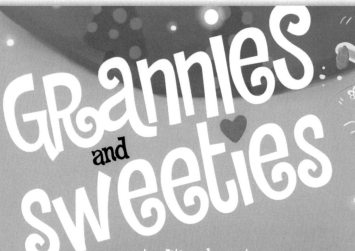

GRannies and sweeties

a non-traditional way to serve
sweet potatoes during the holidays!
(and not a marshmallow in sight!)

ingredients:

* 8 large sweet potatoes,
  scrubbed clean
  and cut into cubes
  DON'T PEEL THEM!

  1" cubes does the trick nicely!

* 3 grannie smith apples,
  cored and cut into cubes
  DON'T PEEL THEM!

* 1/2 cup thinly sliced
  shallots (about 3-4)

* 1/2 cup olive oil

* 1 tsp of EACH:
  cinammon, nutmeg
  cardamon,

* a pinch (OWW!) of:
  kosher salt
  white pepper
  cayenne pepper

* optional but really yummy:
  1/4 cup golden raisins

1. PREHEAT THE OVEN TO 350°
2. In a large bowl, toss all ingredients together until the veggies and fruit are well-coated.

2. Pour onto a large baking sheet, arranging in one layer, so that everything gets cooked uniformly.

3. Bake for 45-1hr. The sweeties should be just soft to the touch and the shallots and grannies caramelized.
3. Serve grannies and sweeties with a holiday bird, and the leftovers make AWESOME pancake add-ins!

Grannies and Sweeties by Colleen Madden from Philadelphia, PA (greenfrographics.com)   39

brussels sprouts

1 and 1/2 pound brussels sprouts
(freshest you can find)

3 tablespoons fresh lemon juice

3 tablespoons extra virgin olive oil

1 teaspoon fresh thyme leaves

salad

DIRECTIONS:

Shred the brussels sprouts whisper thin using a mandoline, or alternately, a knife. Five minutes before serving, place the shredded sprouts in a large mixing bowl and toss gently with the olive oil, lemon juice, thyme, chives, salt, and hazelnuts. Taste and adjust the seasoning, adding more lemon juice if needed, keeping in mind the cheese will bring a salty element to the salad. Add the cheese and toss once or twice to distribute it evenly throughout the salad.
(For a touch of sweetness add some craisins)

1/4 cup hard, salty, aged cheese, shaved

1/3 cup fresh chives, minced

2-3 pinches sea salt

1 1/3 cups hazelnuts, smashed and toasted

(pecorino or parmesan)

©tracymattocks 2011

Brussels Sprouts Salad by Tracy Mattocks from Nashville, TN (tracymattocks.com) 41

Sweet Acorn Squash

You'll need:

- 1 acorn squash
- 2 tbs. butter
- 2 tbs. brown sugar
- 2 tbs. cinnamon

A healthful holiday dish!

Halve squash & remove seeds. Score insides with knife. Add ingredients and bake at 375° f. for about an hour, or until tender.

yum.

Sweet Acorn Squash by Audrey Tate from Phoenix, AZ (audreytate.com)

1 1/2 cups sugar
3/4 cup water
3 whole cloves
3 whole allspice
2 cinnamon sticks
1 12 oz. bag fresh cranberries
zest of 1 orange

Bring sugar, water, cloves, allspice & cinnamon sticks to a boil in a sauce pan. Cook, stirring, until syrup is clear, about 3 minutes. Add cranberries & cook until they begin to pop open, about 5 minutes. Remove from heat, add grated orange zest, & cool. Refrigerate sauce for 1 to 3 days. Take out whole spices before serving.

Cranberry Sauce by Monika Roe from Paso Robles, CA (monikaroe.com)

Soups
& Main Dishes

CRANBERRY OATMEAL

Bring water and cider to boil. ADD Oats and a handful of CRANBERRIES. Simmer and stir until the berries burst!

Cranberry Oatmeal by Jana Christy from North Adams, MA (janachristy.com)

Serves 6.

Wild Mushroom and Chestnut Soup

Melt butter in saucepan with the olive oil
add the garlic, onion and celery, sauté until soft
add mushrooms, white wine, chicken stock & thyme
bring to the boil then simmer for 20 minutes
add the chestnuts and cook for another 5 minutes
Purée soup until smooth, then return soup to pan
Stir in the crème fraîche

Ingredients

2 tbsp butter   2 tbsp Olive Oil

1 Onion Finely Chopped   2 Sticks Of Celery Chopped 2 cups Mixed Wild Mushrooms 1 Clove garlic

2/3 cup White Wine   3¼ cup Chicken Stock Fresh thyme

1 ¾ cup Cooked and Peeled Chestnuts

¾ cup Creme Fraiche

Wild Mushroom and Chestnut Soup by Amanda Dilworth from Derbyshire, UK (amandadilworth.co.uk)

① Mince 1 TBSpoon of ginger & 1 TBSP of garlic

② Chop up one sweet onion.

③ Peel & Chop up 2 pounds of Carrots & one sweet potato.

④ Combine 1⅓ cup plain yogurt, 1 tsp thyme, ½ tsp black pepper & 1 TBSP honey.

by Margaret Hagan

December 2011

Winter Root

52

5. Lightly toast ¼ cup pinenuts over high heat, then cool.

6. Heat up 2 TBSP of olive oil on Med-High, then sweat the onion for 10 min, then stir in garlic + ginger.

7. Add in the carrots, potatoes & 4 cups stock. Simmer til tender.

8. Puree with hand blender, & fold in the nuts & the yogurt mix.

9. Add salt & pepper to taste.

SOUP

Winter Root Soup by Margaret Hagan from Palo Alto, CA (razblint.com)   53

WINTER-WARMER SOUP

1 CHOP
THE ONION & SOFTEN IN EXTRA-VIRGIN OLIVE OIL FOR 10 MINS

2 CHOP
VEGETABLES & THEN ADD
ALL INGREDIENTS INTO A LARGE PAN

3 BOIL
FOR APPROX 20 MINS
OR UNTIL VEGETABLES ARE SOFT

4 BLEND
TOGETHER IN A FOOD PROCESSOR

* 1 BUTTERNUT SQUASH * 1 ONION * 2 RED PEPPERS * 1 LARGE CARROT * SPRINKLE OF GROUND GINGER

...SeRVe...

* PINCH OF SALT AND PEPPER   * 4 CUPS VEGETABLE STOCK

©Sarah Ward 2011

Winter-warmer Soup by Sarah Ward from Sheffield, UK (gingerbred.co.uk)   55

(DUTCH) DOEKE'S WONDERFULL WARM * WINTER SOUP WITH A DROP * OF SNOW WHITE CRÈME FRAÎCHE

yes, that's me!

STEP 1

chop the garlic in very small pieces, and chop the onions in bigger pieces. then; sweat them in 5 minutes with some ~~olif~~ olive oil.

STEP 2

chop up all the carrots and sweat them in the pan with the onions and garlic

How to make?

INGREDIENTS:

1 BAG of CARROTS ✳ [±15 SMALL ONES] ★ ★

2 ONIONS [I PREFER RED]

2 of those GARLIC THINGIES
1 or 2 of those THINGIES ✳
YOU CAN PUT IN IT
SO IT TASTE NICE
1 CUP OF CRÈME FRAÎCHE

SALT & PEPPER
& SOME ★
CHIVES

STEP 3 ✳ ★ ★

put water in it and when it is boiling; put the stock cubes in as well. ★

STEP 4

the organic ones are the best!

(the best part!) taste the soup and put salt and pepper in it if you like. ★ & blend ✳

STEP 5 ✳

yes that's me! (again)
(yes this was só easy)
(serve with a spoon of creme fraiche and some chopped chives!

Wonderful Warm Winter Soup by Doeke Van Null from Zwolle, The Netherlands (flickr.com/photos/doekevn) 57

ROASTED
BUTTERNUT
SQUASH
ASPARAGUS
KALE
FARRO
ROASTED GRAPES

Peel & cube one butternut squash.
Chop 2-3 stems of fresh thyme & rosemary.
Toss squash, herbs, salt & pepper with olive oil
Roast (single layer) for about 20 minutes
in 425° oven.
Toss 10 trimmed asparagus and 12 grapes
with olive oil, spread on baking sheet and
and roast for 10 minutes in 425° oven.
Cook farro according to package.
While farro is still warm combine with all
other ingredients and toss with fresh kale
(cut into small pieces).
Give mixture a squeeze of fresh
lemon juice.
Salt & pepper to taste

Vegetarian Farro by Salli Swindell from Hudson, OH (studiosss.tumblr.com)   59

INGREDIENTS (serves 4)

- 1 tbs extra virgin OLIVE OIL
- ¼ cup LEEKS, white part only
- ½ tsp finely chopped FRESH GARLIC
- 1 LEMON ZEST
- ½ tsp SALT
- ¼ tsp coarse ground BLACK PEPPER
- 1 tbs FRESH PARSLEY, chopped
- 4 WILD KING SALMON FILETS, skinless and boneless

METHOD

1 Preheat oven to 375 degrees F/gas mark 5 2 In a mixing bowl, combine first seven ingredients and mix well 3 Add the SALMON FILETS to the bowl *and* toss until coated 4 Fit a wire rack into a rimmed baking sheet. Place SALMON on top *and* bake for about 12 – 15 mins or until lightly opaque inside 5 Serve with new potatoes *and* fresh green beans 6 Enjoy!

Roasted King Salmon by Sarah-Anne Fielding from Berkshire, UK (nannys-a.co.uk)

'SIZZLE'

FRY ON EACH
SIDE UNTIL
BROWN.

A DASH OF
CREAM

CHOP
these finely

SPRINKLE
OF CRANBERRIES

ADD A DASH
OF SHERRY

MASSAGE A
GOOD QUALITY
BEEF FILLET (1KG)
WITH BUTTER
& SEASON

MUSHROOMS 1.5 CUPS

SHALLOTS 4 OZs.

CHESTNUTS ½ CUP

TARRAGON 1 TBSP

SAUTÉ
all

BLEND

BAKE FOR 20-30 MINS AT 400°F

ROLL OUT SOME PUFF PASTRY, LAY THE BEEF IN THE CENTRE & TOP IT WITH A THICK LAYER OF THE MIX.

BRUSH WITH MILK

FOLD

SEAL WITH A FORK

festive WELLINGTON

Festive Wellington by Laura Callaghan from London, UK (lauralaurapicturedrawer.blogspot.com)

ingredients

3lbs of ground chuck

1/4 cup ground sausage

1/2 cup parsley chopped

1/2 tsp pepper

1/3 cup romano cheese

3 cloves finely chopped garlic

3 eggs

1-1/2 tsp salt

1/4 cup water or milk

3/4 cup italian bread crumbs

-mix all ingredients in a large bowl & form mixture into balls.

-bake at 350 for 40 min.

*if desired, place meatballs into large pot & cover with favorite sauce; simmer for 45 min. on low

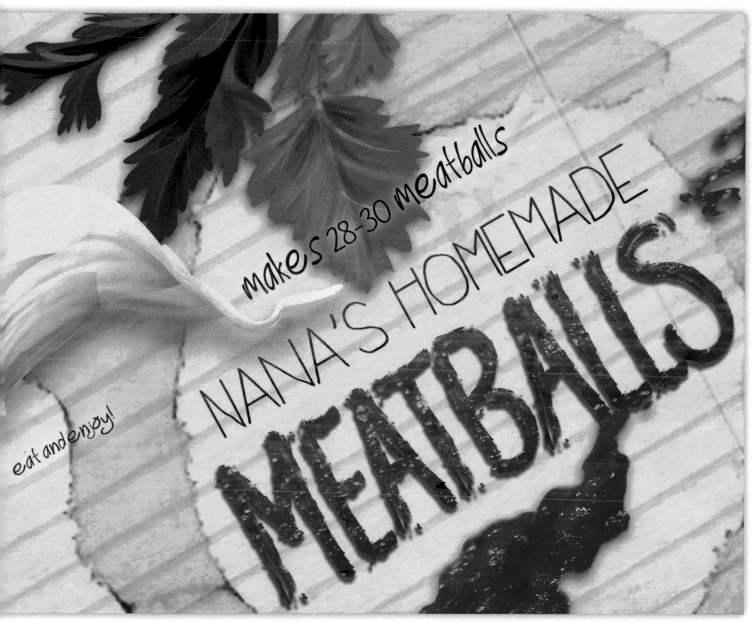

makes 28-30 meatballs

NANA'S HOMEMADE
MEATBALLS

eat and enjoy!

Nana's Homemade Meatballs by Brianna Parrish from Columbus, OH (briannaparrish.blogspot.com)   65

TO A HOT FRYING PAN ADD OIL 2 TSP CUMIN & CORIANDER 1 TSP TURMERIC & CURRY POWDER

SPICES

AFTER TWO MINS

ADD THE PURÉE MIX

COOK FOR 2 MINUTES

FOR THE BEST BASMATI RICE WASH THOROUGHLY. USE TWICE THE AMOUNT OF WATER TO RICE* BRING TO THE BOIL, ADD SALT, TURN HEAT TO LOWEST, COVER WITH TIGHT FITTING LID. 20 MINUTES LATER PERFECT RICE * 2 OZ PER PERSON

AND 2 OZ OF FROZEN BROAD BEANS

ADD 1 TSP GARAM MASALA COOK FOR 10 MINUTES, SERVE WITH LOTS OF FRESH CORIANDER

weef

A very special thanks to all the wonderfully talented illustrators whose recipe artwork appears in this book:

Brooke Albrecht, Nathalie Beauvois, Laura Callaghan, Jean Cameron, Jana Christy, Amanda Dilworth, Sarah-Anne Fielding, Jessica Flannery, Krista Genovese, Lisa Graves, Margaret Hagan, Colleen Madden, Sharon Mann, Kathleen Marcotte, Tracy Mattocks, Brianna Parrish, Miro Poferl, Monika Roe, Alex Savakis, Mayte Sánchez Sempere, Heidi Schweigert, Silvia Sponza, Audrey Tate, Doeke Van Null, Sarah Ward and WEEF

THEY DRAW & COOK.™

Designed & edited by Nate Padavick and Salli S. Swindell
studiosss.tumblr.com

Produced & published by They Draw & Cook
Studio SSS, LLC
13 Steepleview Drive
Hudson, Ohio 44236
theydrawandcook.com